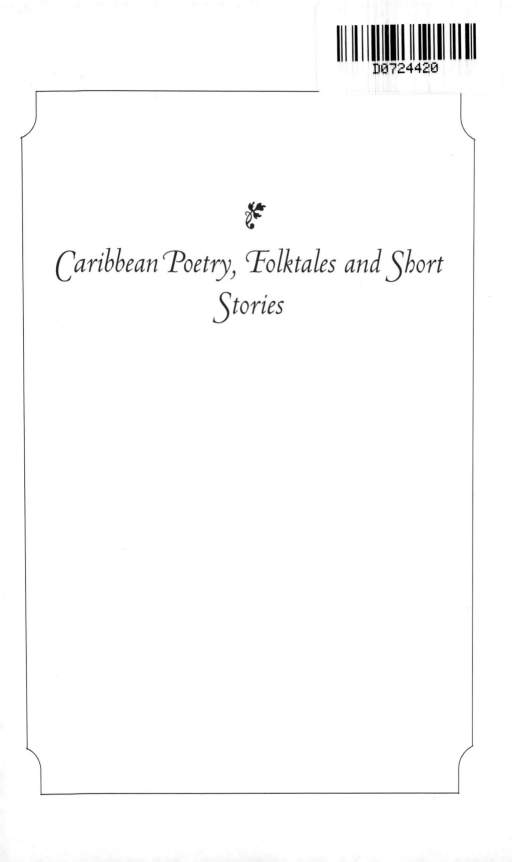

Caribbean Poetry, Folktales and Short Stories

Caribbean Poetry, Folktales and Short Stories

Ophelia A. Powell Torres
Victor M. Torres

iUniverse, Inc.

New York Lincoln Shanghai

Caribbean Poetry, Folktales and Short Stories

iUniverse books may be ordered through booksellers or by contacting:

iUniverse
2021 Pine Lake Road, Suite 100
Lincoln, NE 68512
www.iuniverse.com
1-800-Authors (1-800-288-4677)

ISBN-13: 978-0-595-33257-1 (pbk)
ISBN-13: 978-0-595-78042-6 (ebk)
ISBN-10: 0-595-33257-9 (pbk)
ISBN-10: 0-595-78042-3 (ebk)

Printed in the United States of America

Contents

INTRODUCTION

This book is written for people who love people, enjoy life, like to laugh and share stories to bring humor, comfort and happiness into other peoples' lives.

We would like to thank our friends and families who graciously listened and added to the stories, poetry and folktales written in this book. Thanks to Vernel Powell, Julia Gregoire, Helena Blake, Elaine Hill, Antonio Torres, Victor Torres Jr., for their encouragement, words of wisdom and for believing in us.

The Caribbean Islands are unique and beautiful with similarities and differences. Each island has its own dialect and pronunciation of words. Some words must be spelled the way they are pronounced, the same grammar must be used in order to capture the person the story is about or the person who is telling the story. Each island has its own attractions.

The Caribbean Islands also share similarities with the rest of the world in that the people face the same harsh realities of diseases such as HIV/AIDS, whether in a small or large way.

In the Caribbean, family reunions consists of many stories from the usual story tellers, some of these same stories became the basis of family social gatherings.

We expect that our readers will become familiar with the stories, poetry and folktales which serve as the basis of Caribbean mores and folkways. Stories about Tampo, Savannaire, Edgar, Trigger-Foot and others are ethnic keys into the ways we meld with differences among peoples of the Caribbean. Stories about Crab and Rice, Kalaloo, Souse, Maubi and other tropical drinks give an idea about the condiments, seasonings and herbs that distinguish us or make us similar to peoples of other lands. In the respect of Washington Irving, Icabod Crane gives us insight about story telling in Irving's New York. We would like some younger Caribbean Islanders as well as visitors-old and new alike-to know why we do what we do, why we eat what we eat and why we embrace some parts of the dominant

U.S. culture. For example, in 2004 the United States Virgin Islands Governor, Charles W. Turnbull, enacted into law the term "Qualbe," a mixture of European and African music, as the official music of the U.S. Virgin Islands. This was always the nature of how we see and relate to other cultures. Maypole and Quadrille are basically Irish music and dance. Since the earliest time, people of the Caribbean-Dutch, French, Spanish, Danish, British-have always shared in these borrowings, and thus the title: CARIBBEAN POETRY, FOLKTALES AND SHORT STORIES.

BEAUTY OF A VIRGIN

Untouched, unspoiled, innocent, friendly, natural, soft and gentle
Plush, luscious, soothing, spectacular, magnificent and exotic
Winding roads and panoramic scenic views of sister virgins
Green mountains standing tall and elegant
Dressed in robes of green like a queen
Blue skies give the gin clear waters varying tints of blue and
     aquamarine
Romantic moonlit skies that glitter on pristine waters like diamonds
White sandy beaches massage the soles and relaxes the body and
     mind
Visitors and locals play with schools of fishes, walk and talk with the
     animals
Iguanas stop and nod their heads as if to say, "hello! how are you"?
Even visiting New Yorkers smile and say "Hello."
Visitors can easily forget their woes and worries enjoying this virgin.
Many vacationers come, but never leave.
Would you? Leave "love city"
St. John, United States Virgin Islands?

HISTORICAL/ ANTHROPOLOGIC NOTE

Name calling is an important aspect of culture in the English colonial tropics, a carry-over from English literature, puns, double entendre, word games and a plethora of figurative language, euphemisms which led in part to calypso and are an integral part of the mores and folkways of the Caribbean.

The shear meter and feet of words were enough to amuse the poet, lyricist or calypsonian. "Reptile" sounds different, creative and serves as a metaphor and spur of momentary brilliance that would produce levity. The saying goes "if you can't laugh, if you don't have a sense of humor, you're not alive. You must be able to laugh at yourself or a brunt of humor about you and yours."

UNCLE EDGAR

Uncle Edger was nicknamed "Edgar Bradshaw." But his real name was Edgar Liburd. I never knew why the people called him that name until I grew older and found out he was a big supporter of the late Premier Bradshaw of St. Kitts and Nevis, West Indies. He was such a big fan that he called the Premier: "Papa Bradshaw." However, this story is not about Uncle Edgar's hero, "Papa Bradshaw," but about Uncle Edgar himself.

Uncle Edgar made and sold Hammon Report (moonshine) and planted cotton for a living. In Brown Hill Village, Nevis, cooking Hammon Report was against the law, but Uncle Edgar did not seem to care, he made good money from selling Hammon Report.

Uncle Edgar had been caught by the police several times and each time he was caught his niece Gladys, (nicknamed God-a-Girl for her kindness and beauty), would bail him out of jail. He would always promise to repay with bags of cotton, but never did. Once the bill was paid that would be the last time Uncle Edgar would be seen until he was caught again. The last time Uncle Edgar was caught by the police cooking Hammon he tried to get his bail money from God-a-Girl, but this time her grandmother, Florie Liburd, nicknamed, "Florie Bujunk" stepped in and asked Uncle Edgar about the bags of cotton he owed for his previous bails from jail. Uncle Edgar shouted "Florie Liburd shut up, you reptile." Until this day I don't know why my Uncle Edgar called my grandmother a reptile. Reptiles are cold and dangerous. My grandmother was warm and loving. Maybe he thought my grandmother was cold for not allowing God-a-Girl to pay for his bail that time. I think my grandmother was just fed up with his promises, his Hammon making, cotton picking lies.

CHRISTMAS DINNER

For about six years Crep spent Christmas in the Clock Tower of Fort Christian, the famous Fort with the date on the front, 1671, just above the clock tower. After his thanksgiving dinner there, he was released and went to his home in Savan. Actually he was a guest of the old Queen Louise Home, just above Post Master Ottley. He knew the court docket just as well as any court bailiff. He would watchfully wait until Judge Christian-a transposed judge from our sister island of St. Croix, now practicing on St. Thomas civil court—was on the Bench.

Judge Christian was among the darkest of Negro brothers and Crep thought he would play upon Judge Christian's deep blue-black pigment to anger him with contempt of court and be sentenced to one week in the clock tower of Fort Christian.

As was his habit, he waited until the midst of the case he had carefully selected and entered the courtroom, walked straight down the aisle stopping all rhetoric and when he had gotten the attention; he would accost Judge Christian. He would initiate his tirade with:

"Judge Christian, why in the name of Jesus Christ did God make you so black? I know many black men and women just as black as you, I have seen them work hard and sweat hard. All of them sweat good, regular sweat like everybody else, but you, you're different. You even sweat different."

Judge Christian: "Well Mr. Crep, How am I different. Would you please tell the court?"

Crep: You different because where everybody sweat ordinary, you sweat black ink.

Judge Christian: That does it Mr. Crep. I fine you one week for contempt of court to be served in the clock tower of this Fort Christian, to begin forthwith. Court Officer, please lead Mr. Crep to the Clock Tower. See that he doesn't leave there 'till after Three Kings Day. I am pleased to know, Mr. Crep, that our turkey here at Fort Christian is better than what you get at Queen Louise. I shall pass your complements to the chef.

Crep: The black bastard didn't know that's exactly what I wanted.

THE DRUNKARD
"Inibriated"

Staggering from side to side.

Speaking a new language that no one understands.

Don't know where he is or where he is going.

Don't even know where he comes from or to whom he belongs.

Trying to get somewhere, but going nowhere.

Trying to hold on to something, but there is nothing.

Everything seems to be moving.

Will go anywhere with anyone.

Accepting, crying, dangerous, denying, cursing, laughing.

Everyone becomes his friend as he begs for cigarettes and money

Only to support his pleasure.

Plastered, putting himself in harms way of the lowdown and the
downlow.

Abusive and out of control.

He is thrown into the slammer

Until he is calmer.

He awakens trembling for another fixer upper.

An end must come to his un-bearing leisure

Before his soul burn in hell fire.

THE CHAIN GANG
Crimes go Unpunished

"Abuse without mercy" I called it. I can still envision the horrid beatings those four little boys received from their father as the village people stood by and watched, afraid to tackle this ruthless man (calling himself father) to the ground. Why wouldn't they do something to save the little boys? My little mind was racing at eight years of age.

The village people say the mother of the little boys had died of beatings and mistreatment from her husband, the boys father.

There were no Human Services and Social Workers in my village. I was in elementary school. I was a child. The sorrow in my heart was too much to bear. I am an adult now, but, I still see the chain gang in my minds eye today.

It was a cold drizzly morning about 5:30 a.m. when I was awakened by loud noises in the village. People were running in the streets screaming and crying. I ran with my mother to the streets, only to find four little naked boys with their hands tied in front of them and chain tied around their ankles linked to each other. Their father beat them mercilessly with his thick, long, large leather belt. They screamed in pain and shivered in the early morning cold. It was a pathetic scene. Their charge was that they had not done their chores the night before. Therefore, they were being taken to jail in the Town.

I don't know how far they got, but I know the father and four little boys returned to the village later that day. Someone must have put some sense into the father's head to turn him around. I was hoping the police would lock him up instead for child abuse.

I have grown to realize the father was a sick man with mental health issues and needed help. No one had the insight in those days to realize he was mentally ill.

The irony of the story is that the four boys grew into young adults and their father became very ill and elderly. The four boys took very good care of him until he died. My grandmother would say "once a man twice a child." "The people you hurt on the way up might be the same people you see on the way down."

Always remember as Whitney Houston says "the children are our future."

Take good care of your children, nurture them and love them; they may have to care for you and nurture you one day.

TALES TO LIVE BY

When the left palm of your hand itches it means you will get money

When the right palm of your hand itches it means you will spend money

When the soles of your feet itches it means you will travel afar

When the cock crows in font of the door a visitor is coming from afar

When your left eye twitches you will see someone special

If a black cat crosses the road in front of your path you will have bad luck probably get into an accident if you are driving.

When a donkey brays it means the world is upside-down.

When dogs begin to howl someone in the neighborhood is going to die.

When dogs lie on their backs with their four feet up someone is going to die.

If a green grass-hopper flies into your house, you will get money.

When Ants are marching in a line with white material in their mouths it is the sign of a funeral procession.

Wash the soles of your feet at nights before you go to bed because you may get sick and no-one will have the time to wash your feet before you go to the hospital.

Never fall asleep under the moonlight, you may get up with your mouth twisted.

THE FIVE-PECENTERS

In the nineties, I visited my home, St. Thomas, U. S. Virgin Islands. The story then filling the media waves was about a skyjacking. A flight headed for a federal prison in Washington from the Cyril E. King Airport was diverted to Cuba. The skyjackers begged for political asylum from the Cuban government. It was granted. The plane was directed to return to Cyril E. King. Naturally an investigation was conducted to determine how this skyjacking was carried out. Not many people knew the origin of the circumstances leading to the incarceration. This is that story.

Miscegenation is the phenomenon which gave rise to the mulatta and the various gradation of the darker brother. In St. Thomas, U.S. Virgin Islands, a group of fair-skinned young adults banded together and called themselves "The Five-Percenters."

Their ideology was founded on their perception that they comprised five-percent of the population, as a distinct group. They also felt that they were entitled to five percent of the jobs; they were entitled to five percent of whatever wealth was to be distributed. Some of them were unemployed and unemployment was the glue that bonded them. But a dark-skinned darker brother was the force behind the bond. These youngsters were a potentially aggressive group. They had no headquarters to speak of. They met around Pearl M. Pearson Gardens and later around the Oswald "Skinny" Harris Court," a housing development similar to Pearl M. Pearson Gardens. They ambled around Lockhart's Garden, Sugar Estate and Wheatley Mall. These developments were within a square mile radius.

Darky—we shall call him—an older Cruzian, who had lived in New York City and tasted deep of the Jewish ire appointed himself their leader. He was the Arthur Dubin/Woodrow Wilson for this group. He appealed to their sense of adventure and their sense of fair play. I often wondered if the Five-percenters could have been casted as communist; their ideology was similar. It was the occasion of the second speech Darky had made to these young men.

With no headquarters, no structure, no particular plans, they hit the country road on foot, not rowdy or menacing, and found themselves facing a house under which there was parked for the night a Dodge Colt. Whenever I think back on the circumstances with Darky present on this fateful night, I always ask myself some questions. What were they after? What were their plans?

The conversation that ensued is not a diversion or digression. It helps to pin point the complicity of the Darker brother.

"This is where Alan Grammer Lives. This is the racist. He used to own a restaurant and lost his liquor license for refusing to sell to a black man. He lost this license in court. Judge Gordon took it away from him. Now he has a music store. Let's burn his car."

The smoke from the burning car awakened the Grammer Family. Mr. Grammer moved toward the smoke to investigate. Grammer called some of the boys by name. Some of them were musicians as was the darker brother. The darker brother was recognized and called by name for he was a bass player and had made purchases in Grammer's Music Store on Radaats Gade. If I am not mistaken, Kelsey was a four-year-old toddler then.

Unknown to the group as a whole, Arthur Niles was packing. Without warning Niles pulled out his pistol and shot Grammer who died within the hour.

The Daily News could corroborate some of the following. Niles after 24 hours on the loose, turned himself in to Police Officer Leerdam, well-known as son of a Special Delivery Postman. Was Leerdam Fair enough to be a Five-Percenter?

The St. Thomian powers that be directed Niles future. Whether the Legislature, the St. Thomas Men's Club, the Office of the Governor, the families of the Five-Percenters, or others, two College of the Virgin Islands professors of psychology were ordered to examine Niles and produce findings—for the record—that would cause Niles to be found "Guilty by Insanity" and remanded to a booby hatch in Washington rather than do hard time in Christiansted Penitentiary or a U.S. Federal Prison.

Feeling very vulnerable and ordered to act against their consciences the Psychologists left the Virgin Islands. They concurred on one thing: That Niles was crazy in just one area on thinking.

The trial of Niles provided information to arrest some of the Five-Percenters who were also sentenced because of the Grammer's death. These were the ones being transported to a federal prison when the skyjacking occurred diverting the scheduled flight to Cuba.

The grapevine has it that Five-percenters working at the Cyril E. King Airport planted the firearms used in the skyjacking. Were the powers to be—those listed vide infra—involved in the skyjacking? I often wonder if Curtis Callendar and other Virgin Islanders familiar with the court case have seen any relationship between Grammer's wrongful death and the lost of his liquor license. This was an unnecessary lost of life and undeserved suffering to his wife and three children.

UNCAPTURED TIME

We grow up to be grandmothers
How and when did all this happened
Time seems to pass by so quickly
Work hard, play hard
Sleepless nights, yet school work to get done
Producing, supporting families
All in a days work
Leaving the most important things unnoticed.
One day before your very eyes
Sons and daughters grown and
married with children of their own.
Grandchildren calling grandma!
Looking around for confirmation
There is no other adult but me.
My two grandchildren laughing and jumping in the pool
Showing off their gymnastic and swimming skills.
Grandma is now a security guard, a life guard
making sure that everything and everyone is safe.
Pondering how time flies and roles change.
Take time to watch the roses grow from tiny buds to blooming
    flowers.
Time never stand still, but passes into eternity never to be recaptured.

BUSH "SLY" MONGOOSE

Mama, my grandmother, had her old friend Edwardo. Papa was still around, but the rhum sweetened his tongue; he was little use to Mama. Edwardo became "the man around the house" and jumped at Mama's every whim.

Edwardo had the brick oven in the yard up to par. He built Mama an ice-box which became a coal bin. He kept the fence in panes, the gate hinged and performed a variety of other chores. During the evening when Mama fancied some Rosenblum or tobacco, Edwardo fetched it. "Wardo" was his everyday name.

Wardo's past was checkered. In his fifties he had resorted to supplying Mama with chicken, eggs and regularly he had become adept at supplying Mama with tanya, yam, sweet-potato, corn, okra not to mention sour-sap, sugar-apple, custard-apple, mangoes, in or out of season.

Papa spent most of his able hours at Bar Normandie in French Town. Many women tried to drop a dime on "Wardo" about Mama, but Mama stayed the course like Lady Godiva. One day Papa came home and found Wardo plucking a chicken. Wardo already had the reputation of being seen close-by, but missing when anything was missing. An angry Papa questioned Wardo about his newest plucking. Before Wardo got a word out, Papa yelled loudly: "Where is my goddam cut-lash." Wardo was through the Gate heading North. Someone gave Papa his cut-lash and the run was on, Wardo with a fifty yard head start.

Among the many epithets Papa yelled at Wardo is the infamous "Bush Mangoose" or "Sly Mangoose," the title of one of St. Thomas most famous calypsos.

TRIGGER FOOT WIDER

My cousin Wider had a distinct click in her left knee when she walked. The click was very audible, plus the back of her knee would bend backwards out of alignment with her back and spine as if she had a wooden leg.

Wider was beautiful with long flowing silky black hair. She thought her trigger foot was a draw-back from young handsome men being attracted to her. She would try her best to walk straight and maintain a good posture to try to avoid the trigger knee from clicking especially when she saw a handsome man. 'She thought she was people.' She would confirm with me as to whether the left knee was straight or not. I was not planning to disappoint her, she was trying too hard to get a husband. So, each time she asked me if she was walking straight, I would say "yes". Naturally I was fibbing through my teeth. I was trying to be merciful even though her left knee continued to bend backwards and the clicking never stopped. It even appeared to sound louder since she was trying to straighten up her left foot.

I was so happy when a young handsome man name Mr. Willy, ignored Widers' clicking knee and fell in love with her. He loved her for her beauty and proposed marriage. Mr. Willy and cousin Wider had a beautiful wedding.

Widers' new husband Mr. Willy was as merciful to her as I was. When people questioned if the clicking trigger knee annoyed him, he failed to respond and until today Mr. Willy still parries the question.

MIND OVER BODY

Sitting on the patio at the Divi Carina Bay Hotel, St. Croix, VI.
Engrossed in the gifts of mother nature
The breeze soothing, flowers blooming, the trees
swaying in the wind from the beautiful Caribbean sea.
White clouds moving gently across the soft blue skies.
At a distance one can hear the rhythm of melodious Caribbean
    calypso music.
The waves from the ocean massaging the beautiful white sandy beach
and caressing the coral reefs
Mesmarizing, more powerful than a sleeping pill
I slowly fall asleep.
Awaking I feel refreshed and energetic
Ready to take on the challenges of the day.

THE BURNING MAN

In Brown Hill Village all the people looked out for each other especially if there were a crisis. Even if they had disagreements and were not speaking to each other, they would still come to each other's aide.

Sun Bumba ran errands for the people of Brown Hill Village. That was his job. A messenger-man.

One day, Tanto Jack sent Sun Bumba to buy Hammon Report (a rum similar to moonshine). As usual Bumba stopped to talk to everyone he met on the road and he was late returning with the Hammon Report. Tanto Jack was so angry ("in a passion"), he opened the bottle of Hammon, dounced it all over Bumba, lit a match and threw it on Bumba. Needless to say, one hundred and fifty proof rum and flames do not go together. Bumba instantly ignited in flames. He started running all over the place, screaming "Oh me God, Tanto Jack bun me up." By the time the women in the village caught up with Bumba, 80 percent of his body was already burnt. He had second and third degree burns all over his body. The women threw cold water on Bumba and wrapped him in blankets and sheets. Feeling sorry for Bumba, thinking he was going to die, the women of the village prayed for him and told him to pray to God. They should have told Bumba what to say to God when he prayed, because Bumba did not know how to pray. Bumba began to shout repeatedly, "Lard a lang a gine, a lang a gine." He too thought he was going to die. I remember Ms. Clark saying, "Bumba's teeth was playing organ." He fell while running and had broken and loosened some of his teeth.

That night I watched the ambulance take my friend Bumba away to the hospital. "Was Bumba really dying"? I asked myself? I was too young to understand. I thought about not being able to get into BumBa's house to jump on his bed. I also thought about the ground provisions under his bed and the dried meat hanging on the outside of his house. What will the people in the village say when they find out.

Bumba returned home from the hospital several weeks later. He had lots of scars about his body. He never returned to Tanto Jack's house.

RUN! BLACK WOMAN! RUN!

Your life is in danger.
Your black man is "under cover"
He is definitely looking for a killer
"Kickin" doors to find a fairy lover.
"Mixing things" that don't even go together.
"Messing around" in places that cause people to wonder
People questioning, are they right for each other?
Leaving you to ponder.
Is he bisexual, gay, yet calling himself a straight lover?
He shows no signs of effeminate behavior.
Black man come out of the closet and state your case
Black woman life is at stake.
Black woman, look for clues in the eyes of your macho lover.
The eyes say a lot.
Is he saying where he is, where he is not?
Making you believe it is another woman and plans to tie the knot?
Puzzled and confused, mind and body on the go.
Like a detective you peer in windows and around corners to find a
    clue.
Alas! That lowdown black man is on the 'downlow'
Run black woman run.

BRU TOKOMA — THE DOG &
BRU ANANSI — THE CAT WHY
DOGS HATE CATS — THE
DUMPLIN TREE

When dogs and cats were friends, they did and shared everything. While strolling together they passed a private estate and noticed that some of the dumplins on the dumplin tree had ripened. Bru Tokoma couldn't squeeze through the fence, but Bru Anansi could. They both decided that Bru Anansi would climb the tree and toss the ripe dumplins down to Bru Tokoma and later they would share the dumplins.

When Bru Anansi got close to the tree, he noticed that the fragrance from the dumplins was so strong that he couldn't resist the temptation to eat one. After eating the first dumplin Bru Anansi continued to eat more until he had eaten all the ripe ones. Bru Tokoma was watching him eat the dumplins and was yelling and jumping around: he was fuming. All his anxiety did Bru Tokoma no good. Bru Anansi had eaten them all.

Bru Anansi got so fat and heavy that he couldn't hold himself in the tree. He slid down and thumped on the ground. Now he is too fat to squeeze back through the fence. Bru Anansi thought that Bru Tokoma was so anxious to see him, his good old buddy. What Bru Anansi didn't know was that Bru Tokoma was so angry that he was just very anxious to get his hands on Bru Anansi's throat. Bru Anansi kept apologizing, but to no avail. Bru Tokoma wasn't having any explanation especially not on an empty belly. Finally after several days, even when dumplins were falling, Bru Anansi still failed to give Bru Tokoma even a piece of a dumplin, Bru Anansi could squeeze through the lads of the fence.

By this time all Bru Tokoma could think of was Bru Anansi's throat. Knowing of Bru Tokoma's ire as Bru Anansi squeezed through the fence Bru Tokoma was after him with murder in his mind, his eyes and his heart. Even today Bru Tokoma has never forgiven Bru Anansi for eating all the dumplins. When ever a dog sees a cat, the dog remembers how Bru Anansi allowed Bro Tokoma to starve while he got fatter and fatter.

NEIGHBORHOOD PEEPING TOM

In the village Narco, all the women were mothers to all the children, and all the men were fathers to all the children. All the girls were my sisters and all the boys were my brothers. "It was a family affair in the olden days" as my grandmother Bessie would say. It seems that no matter where I was in the village, Ms. Hiss could see me, but I could never see her. At times, passing on the road close to Ms. Hiss's house, I would hear a voice saying "watch yourself" but I never saw anyone. I Became so accustomed to the sound of the voice that I knew it was Ms. Hiss. My mother Sylvia would know everything I did and everyone I spoke to on the street, even though we had no telephones during those olden days. She would get all the melay from Ms. Hiss. Now-a-days I tend to believe we had invisible runners strictly to carry melay during the olden days.

When my sister Delia and I were growing up in Narco village, Ms. Hiss would always find the opportunity to remind us never to go out after dark and no matter where we were we should try to get home before sunset because "women lose their senses at night" I always wondered what those words meant. Were they meant to frighten us? I was always able to do my home-work in front of the lantern at nights and never once lost my senses. As I grew older those words boggled my mind and whenever I ask Ms. Hiss what the words meant, she would always say: "you will find out when you get older." I am older and wiser now and have put my own interpretation to those words. The night is dark, young girls walking in the darkness, in a village with no electricity, put themselves in harms way of rapists, alcoholics etc." I believe her words, as a mother, were meant not only to frighten us, but also to protect us.

THE BLACK CAT

While many people think black cats are cuddly and friendly and want them as pets, there are others who think they have a bad omen and don't want them around.

In the West Indian culture, black cats symbolize danger and bad luck. If a black cat crosses the road in front of someone while walk or driving, that person may end up in a bad accident or have some bad luck.

Iza wanted to move her wooden shack from next to the water pond. She wanted to move further up the road where life was better and no one would tease her about her big sore foot. She decided to hire Gondin's truck to move her house. The house was slowly lifted and rested on Gondin's flat bed truck and Iza took off to her new location up the road. But, on her way, Iza met with some misfortune when a black cat ran across the street in front of Gondin's truck. Immediately, Iza demanded that Gondin turn the truck around and take her wooden house back to its old location. Gondin did exactly as Iza asked. He turned around and landed the wooden house exactly where he took it from. Iza did not want any bad luck.

The old neighbors laughed at Iza, but the laughing did not matter as long as she felt safe. Life long stories have a way of playing games with people's minds.

CARING

Touch me
Hold me
Look me straight in the eyes and love me.
I am the same person when you caressed me.
I still need your love and advice to guide me
Have I changed so much that you cannot love me?
Believe in me
Look inside me
Trust me
Share your energy with me
So that I can feel strength and passion within me.

MY FRIEND BUMBA

Sun Bumba was a very tall, slinky man. He lived alone in a small wooden shack that rested on four rocks. He had no ground provisions planted, but he always ate the best ground provisions. (tanyas, yams, sweet potatoes, okras, etc).

One day my friends and I (8 years old) were jumping on Bumba's bed. We took pride in the bouncing up and down. We were puzzled as to why the bed would not bounce this time. Our bed at home bounced very easily. We were inquisitive, so we decided to look under Bumba's bed only to find piles of ground provisions so high that they prevented the bed from bouncing. Where did the provisions come from? We wondered.

Bumba usually did meanial tasks for the neighbors and he had very little money. When Bumba caught us peering under his bed, he would say very softly, "Ok Seckie, it is time for you all to go home now."

Another puzzling thought, Bumba had no animals in the pasture, but he always had lots of fresh meat and corned meat hanging on the outside of his house. He ate very well. As my friends and I grew older, we found out Bumba was steeling the provisions from the nearby farm and hiding them under his bed. He was stealing animals from the pasture and slaughtering them for meat, but was never caught. It seems as if Bumba had a sixth sense that would alert him that owners were on the prowl.

Suddenly, one day, Bumba became a shoemaker. He repaired shoes for people in the village. He repaired my school shoes. He replaced the heels with pieces of bee-ltire (automobile tire). It was so roughly done and my shoes became so heavy that they impeded my walking. I Remember when I wore my shoes they would fall off my heels as if I were wearing flappers. The heaviness of the shoes would also hurt my back and made me very tired. Bumba would sometimes wear his customer shoes after he repaired them.

One day, Mantero gave Bumba a pair of shoes to repair. Someone in America had sent him some worn down shoes. Bumba told Mantero to return for the shoes in two days.

Each time Mantero went to Bumba's house to collect his shoes, Bumba's door would be locked from the inside. That is because Bumba already saw Mantero coming and locked himself inside the house.

One day Mantero knocked on Bumba's door, "I know you are in there," he said, "come out, I want my shoes" Bumba did not answer the door, he waited and peeked through a little hole from inside the wooden house until Mantero left and was out of sight before he opened the door and came outside. That same afternoon, Bumba dressed himself and strolled across the street wearing Mantero shoes he received from America.

Here comes Lukie, who yelled out, "Sun Bumba aint those Mantero shoes you have on your feet"? "Take them off right now before I call Mantero," Bumba replied "OK Seckie (Bumba called everybody Seckie or Second) you don't have to tell everyone about the shoes." Bumba was so embarrassed, he returned home and took off Mantero shoes. Mantero did not have to pay Bumba for repairing the shoes; his payment came from wearing the shoes.

TORCHING CRAB

Crabs, blue crabs, large ones are considered a delicacy in St. Thomas, Virgin Islands. As desirable as lobster is as another delicacy, Blue Crab and rice achieve a characteristic flavor that no other food can. If you attempted to cook lobster and rice or any other food considered a delicacy with rice, they fall far short of the unusually rich flavor of crab, not just any crab, just Blue Land Crab.

If you've tried Snow Crab and rice, Rock Crab and rice, Alaskan King Crab and rice or Indigenous Crab and Rice, they may absorb flavor from condiments, herbs and seasoning, but no other crab can compete with Blue Land Crab and rice for its uniqueness and desirability in taste.

Beside male and female crabs, crabs have no important distinctions that add or subtract from their sort-after flavor. They do have three differences. Some have the larger gundy (claw) on the right side and some have it on the left side. The ones with the larger gundies are usually males.

The crabs with the two small gundies are brown and usually female. They don't have as much meat as the blue males with the one large gundy.

Crab forage after sundown and their main diet consists of insects and leaves. They are herbivorous as well as insectivorous. After a deluge or a planters rain crabs leave their holes and may crawl a score or more feet. As their sense of direction is poor, if they wander too far away from their holes, they may not find their way back to their original holes. They may enter any hole into which they may fit and start a fight for possession. Other crabs may invade holes they have just repossessed, in which case there is a fight or they may spend the night burrowing another hole. Sometimes they run into conflicts with large rats. Foraging is not the only reason for leaving the hole. Mating is another reason for leaving the hole. During their mating season females leave a trail of pheramones which drive the male into a frenzy. He then enlarges the hole if she has not already done so and mates. Frequently female crabs are found filled with yellow eggs which is one of the main keys to the characteristic flavor, but you add eggs only to the rice after it is cooked.

Usually female crabs deposit eggs in the heart of coconut trees, the reason crabs inhabit coconut groves, but only if the tree leans over water or a pond and sometimes into the open sea. If a desirable coconut tree is unavailable females seek another tree which may accommodate a nest-like area at the top, or the female makes a make-shift bed upon which she deposits her eggs and leaves them to hatch on their own. Like roaches, when crabs hatch they fall into the pond water and like turtles they head for the rocky coast and spends their first months hunting small insects around the rocky sea. Young crabs grow up to an inch in length, may live in burrows at the surf, for they are amphibious until the age of about two months old. Then they move to the pond area and begin to burrow in sandy areas close to the pond or the sea, most frequently by the pond which usually abounds in insects of their diet. Just like turtles they are vulnerable to the same predators: rats, birds, fishes, mongoose, dogs and cats. If they wander out to the sea which they do and can, they may become food for lobsters, hedgehogs (puffer or blowfish) and pot fish, parrotfish, goutou, wenchman, grunt and various other hard mouth fishes. It would behoove crab lovers to pioneer a program to capture the entire brood of newly hatched crabs and rear them like turtle conservationists do. The madness of egg-laying by the crab has as its protector a wasp nest, or several wasps nests. Usually anyone seeking coconuts will get stung before getting to the crab nest or nests. If there are wasps nests there are crab nests. Also rats lay nests in the hearts of coconut trees, so anyone climbing a coconut tree may very likely bump into one or more nests.

Crab hunting is called torching. A torch may be a flambeau, a bottle containing kerosene, benzene or other slow burning fuel the mouth of which contains a wick made of any piece of dry rag. A torch may consist of a 24 inch piece of a tree branch to which a rag soaked in benzene or kerosene is attached. A flash light of high power is a most effective torch because a blinded crab is an easy prey. Crab hunters use a gunny sack and push a captured crab into the sack. After several males have been placed in a bag or gunny sack, you can hear the larger males breaking the backs of the smaller males or the females.

The mixture of experienced and inexperienced crab hunters make for big fun. See the inexperienced crab's torcher(s) jump and run away from a crab as it raises its large gundy in a threatening gesture to ward off or warn off the inexperienced crab hunter.

Two events cap the crab hunt. The first is a cookout. We carried Pork'n Beans, Bullee Beef with whole kernel corn or early June Peas (petit pois) or Franco American Spaghetti, spam, bread, soda and sanitary plates, cups and napkins. The second event was purging the crabs to rid them of any toxins that may be harmful. To us, then the 'piece de resistance' is the crab and rice. Getting the meat from the legs and the area attached to the legs is an art of much pride. Little stainless steel hooks and forks have been designed to help the intrepid. The flavor and fun are derived from sucking the meat from the legs in one whole piece. If you persist, careful sucking sometimes pull the piece intact straight down the esophagus sometimes choking even the expert. Getting the meat out whole-in one piece-and balling your chime of crab with a spoonful of rice is worth the effort of torching and eating. Removing the back, mouth parts and interals is another trick which could add to the fun.

The preparation of crabs brings the family together like no other culinary event. Even the smallest child becomes enthused at the crustacean. The unusual eyes—like no other animals—is a source of amazement.-*

REFLECTIONS

Strong as an Ox
Vibrant and energetic as a Leo
Bullying at times;
taking long strides across
the pasture to attend her animals,
using her hoe and fork
to plough the land,.
She planted fruit trees, vegetable seeds,
provision slips, pigeon peas and bell peppers.
She worked hard.
The soil was rich and yielded large and sumptuous
yams, potatoes, cabbages lettuce and okras,
carrots and peppers to feed her family.
Her children were healthy and strong and
never missed a day of school. As a matter
of fact they turned out quite well:
manager, teacher, professor, nurse, social worker and
business-woman to name a few.
The years went by so rapidly;
life seems to be slipping away.
The times had taken a toll on her
She sat in her wheel-chair nodding
on and off.
Suddenly I heard:
"Is the lady staying here or is she leaving?"

"What lady I asked.?"
She pointed to the mirror on the wall.
I looked closely to see reflections of my mother in the
mirror.
"Mama! I said, that is you in the mirror."
She smiled, then hung her head in sorrow.
"That lady look so poorie; she could
not be Mirie."

JANCO: THROWING STONES

In the old days children were warned not to throw stones if they had glass windows. During that time the old people use to say, "If you throw a stone behind your back and never look back, you will never return to the place you left behind."

When Janco was leaving Nevis, British West Indies for Tortola, British Virgin Islands, he swore never to return. On his way to St. Kitts, British West Indies on the ferry boat he threw a stone behind him and never looked back. When he boarded the airplane in St. Kitts to Tortola he never looked back at his little island Nevis. He had so many bad memories of being poor, and wearing hand-me-down clothes that he never wanted to go back to Nevis. When he arrived in Tortola everything seemed similar to Nevis, but the people referred to him as "Alien" and "Garrot" from up the island. The people were unfriendly and unkind. Things were bad, worst than Nevis. Back in Nevis, even though he was poor and wore hand-me-downs, he was never hungry and the people were kind and friendly and no one called him names he did not understand. He longed to return home to his little island Nevis where there were plenty of fruits, vegetables, sugarcane, fish and ground provisions. A neighbor or a relative would always offer food if he was hungry. Hunger was never an issue.

In Tortola no one gave him anything. He had to do menial work like cutting yards and cleaning the streets to earn a meager salary. Living accommodations were deplorable. The roof of the little shack where he lived leaked during the rain fall. He had no electricity and had to use a lantern at nights. He had no stove and fridge, thus he cooked on three stones as a make-shift fireplace. He could hardly buy food, thus he did not need a fridge. He had no friends and he was lonely. He yearned to return to Nevis.

Remembering he had thrown the stone behind his back, vowing never to return to Nevis he was afraid to return home. Moving back would break the spell he had cast by throwing the stones behind him and bad things may happen to him. He carried this burden for years while he lived in misery and loneliness in Tortola.

Janco finally muster up the courage to return to his homeland, Nevis. The first time he retuned to Nevis he fell and fractured his arm. Fearing that the spell was still active he quickly returned to Tortola. Years passed and he returned to Nevis a second time only to be beaten up by some young men in the village who did not know him. So he returned to Tortola. Years passed, still longing to return to Nevis, he returned a third time only to become very ill with a fever of 103 degrees fahrenheit. This time he was certain the spell was still active, so he returned to Tortola. Years passed and Janco was now elderly and wanted to spend his last days in his homeland, Nevis. It did not matter if he died on his next return. He would rather to be buried in Nevis. He decided to take his last and final chance to return home a fourth time, but he was still a little fearful. Janco is now living back in Nevis and he is very happy. He is sure now that the spell had been broken after three consecutive incidences. "Three strikes and you are out" so he thought.

The irony of this short story is that you "never throw away the old for the new, because you never know if the new will be better."

JUST THE OTHER DAY
Multidimentional

I was young and frolicky
Running through the pastures
The wind in my hair and face
I hear laughter of children
All around me birds chirping,
      mongoose squeeking, cocks crowing,
      donkeys braying, cattle mooing.
I had not a care
I could spread my wings
The world was mine
I could run for miles and not get tired
I was on a plateau
Then I was transcended to another dimension
I was evolving
Soon I saw myself as wife, mother
I had responsibilities
My children are listening to the same
      stories my mother once told me
My high is not declining
I am on another plane
I have grown wiser
Life and times have afforded me

experience and knowledge to share
I am multidimentional.

EDEN BROWN ESTATE: BEAUTY AND MYSTERY

Eden Brown Estate is a historical slave sugarcane plantation on the island of Nevis, British West Indies. The owners have passed on and the estate was left to perish in the storms and hurricanes of the Caribbean islands. The structures on the estate were never refurbished. According to islanders, the story is that native Nevisians are afraid to visit and refurbish the Structures because people have heard the sound of a woman crying, but the woman was never seen.

The history behind this crying woman is that a love triangle involving two brothers and one woman occurred at Eden Brown Estate in the 1800's. The woman was the lover of one of the brothers and was to be married, but she also fell in love with the other brother and was courting the two brothers at the same time. The brothers challenged each other to a dual to see which one would win and get the woman. One brother was killed and the other died later from wounds he suffered as a result of the dual, just like Alexander Hamilton in his dual with Aaron Burr. Needless to say the woman was left manless. The woman stayed on at Eden Brown estate and wallowed in self pity, pain, sorrow and a broken heart. She later died an old-maid. Her ghost stayed on to haunt Eden Brown estate and the ghost has been crying since the 1800's.

As far back as I can remember, beginning 1953, the then owner of Eden Brown estate was Mr. Mitchel Huggins. Mr. Huggins rode a big white horse from the mountain to the sea that was the extent of Eden Brown Estate. He was my mother's best friend. He used to ride his big white horse to Brown Hill to visit my mother Miriam.

As children, my sisters, brothers and I spent many weekends, summers and holidays at Eden Brown Estate. I remember playing with Labordie and the Sutton

Brothers in the neighborhood. I remember playing with Cook (I don't remember his correct name, but I am trying to find him), whose mother worked at Eden Brown as a chef (and what a chef she was. I don't remember her name either. As children, we used to pick the fruits and chased the chickens and rode with Mitchell Huggins on his big white horse. We took turns riding on the horse or three of us would ride at the same time while Mitchell Huggins guided the horse. We would go down to the beach and pick whelks, swim and run all over the beach.

During my times at Eden Brown estate, none of my family, friends or Mitchell Huggins have ever heard or seen a ghost rampaging through the estate and we never heard the cries of a woman.

I visit Nevis very often and I always visit Eden Brown Estate. It brings back so many fond memories for me. Even with its broken down house and other slave ruins, I still think it is one of the most beautiful estates on the island of Nevis. I listen carefully to hear the woman crying and look for any signs of ghost shadows, but all I see is beauty all around me from mountain to sea. I imagine I hear laughter of children playing. I imagine riding a great big white horse, but I cannot even imagine seeing or hearing a ghost.

Is it a real ghost or people's imagination? In reference to the crying woman I can conclude with this Nevisian slogan "Want all, get none tall" Always be satisfied with what you have.

If I only had money, I could turn Eden Brown Estate into a more beautiful place.

ARCHIE'S PLIGHT

Archie graduated from high school and was now in college majoring in business administration. Archie studied very hard and got A's and B' on all his exams and papers. He was doing well. Archie was sure he would find a good high paying job once he graduated from college, especially since he did his internship with one of the major corporations in the city. Archie graduated just after the 911 disaster. All the companies were downsizing or closing. There were no jobs to be had. Interviews after interviews. In state and out of state. The few companies that had jobs wanted people with experience. Things were bad. Archie began to get weary and depressed. He was angry because college had failed him. One year passed and Archie still did not find employment. He finally landed a job paying minimal wages, but Archie was happy; he was now working. No one in Archie's family—his teachers or professors—had prepared Archie for the real world. College prepared people for the workforce, but college do not guarantee employment.

What major companies do not realize is that young and vibrant college graduates may not have years of experience, but they have a lot to offer. They are stimulating, interesting and energetic. They learn the newest technological advancement. They are excellent advocates with quick minds and always willing to try new things and make new changes. They learn excellent customer service skills and can be great assets to major companies. "An educated mind is a terrible thing to waste"

JUDGE THIELEY

Judge Thieley was a white-haired judge, a carry over from Danish Rule at 1917. He gained a fond reputation as the $2 .00 judge.

A local bullee, going-for-bad gave a sound thrashing, or "dusting off to a smaller, more intellectual teaser. The smaller victim charged the bullee with Aggravated Assault. The bullee was arrested and faced the $2.00 judge, Judge Thieley.

Judge Thieley acknowledged the case and summoned the litigants. Mr. Carlton, you are charged by Mr. Clabidough with Aggravated Assault. How plead you? What? Mr. Carlton responded. The judge rephrased the question. "Did you give Mr. Clabidough a 'good bustarsing?" Of course I did and I would do it again if he repeats his bullshit. That man is a goddam son-of-a-bitch

Watch your language Mr. Carlton. I don't want to fine you for contempt of court.

What? Mr. Carlton Yelled.

How do you plead? Guilty or not guilty, said Judge Thieley.

After much ado, Mr. Carlton said "not guilty" Mr. $2.00.

What did you say? The Judge asked.

'Nothing two,' said Mr. Carlton.

Judge Thieley: Explain your situation.

Mr. Carlton: Well I was walking through the Emancipation Garden and heard someone yell real loud: "Carlton, you go down town for lunch."

The judge responded, I fail to see how being reminded that you go downtown for lunch justifies you jumping on poor little Mr. Clabidough and changing his eye; raising the gulf-ball lump on his forehead not to mention countless bruises, contusions and loss of time from his job on the night soil van. I go downtown for lunch at least 3 to 4 days a week.

The Bailiff asked permission to approach and define for Judge Thieley what he would be doing if he went "down town for lunch."

Judge Thieley yelled, admonishing Mr. Carlton, What? Nasty man. I find you guilty of Aggravated Assault and fine you $2.00.

$2.00 JUDGE — COWBOY (1)
GARRY COOPER

Edwin Gunfit was a tall man, 45 years of age chronologically, but 6 years old mentally. He favored Garry Cooper, an equally tall, well known Western Cowboy. Eddie loved Garry Cooper and answered to no other name. Furthermore, he is never without his flashy gunbelt with two revolvers, Brand name Sheriff.

Mr Wiggley, Bailiff: The court is now in session. The Honorable Judge Thieley presiding. The court will now hear the case of Mr. Par Salmonius versus Mr Edwin Gunfit.

Thieley: Both litigants are present? I have read both complaints and responses. Would both litigants come foward.

Mr. Par Salmonius: Present Your Honor.

Thieley: Mr. Edwin Gunfit?

Bailiff: Your Honor, this litigant's elevator doesn't reach the upper floors. He responds only to the name "Garry Cooper from the Western Front."

Judge Thieley: Mr. Garry Cooper from the Western Front, would you please come forward?

Garry Cooper: Yes your Honor; Garry Cooper from The Western Front, front and center.

JUDGE THIELEY: Mr. Garry Cooper from the Western Front, Mr. Salmonius charges you with Aggravated Assault and Battery.

GARRY COOPER: Wha da mean?

JUDGE THEILEY: Have you ever seen this man (;pointing to Mr. Par Salmonius).

GARRY COOPER: Yes Sir. He's always frigging me up, calling me nasty names.

JUDGE THIELEY: 'If you are found guilty of this crime you may be sent to Christiansted Penetentiary. How do you plead: Guilty or not guilty?

GARRY COOPER: I doan know wha da mean. If you want to find out if ah bust his arse, Yes! I bus his arse

JUDGE THIELEY: Please tell the court—tell me—what happened.

GARRY COOPER: Well Sir, I heard a voice that I know calling Garry Cooper, you're an antiman. I didn't know where the voice was coming from. Then Mr. Ezra Giant Flowers motioned—on the sly—in the direction of Salmonius. Salmonius was saying a nasty ting bout anti Leo 'n me. Then he say I was a homo.

JUDGE THIELEY: Well Mr Garry Cooper, provocation is no excuse to break the law or take the law into your own hands.

GARRY COOPER: Sir, Your Honor Sir; you only say that because there is more money for the court in this type of case. If/n I brung a case to you bout name callin—just like Salmonius calling me antiman, you would find some way to trow ouk the case, hit that ol wood hammer on your counter and yell: Case dismiss."

JUDGE THIELEY: "Why don't you try such a complaint some time and test the court. The court can't give you satisfaction when you are the one breaking the law. Try to be a bit on the righteous side in the future. Mr. Salmonius, did you call out in an annoying tone any derogatory or slanderous names at Mr.Garry Cooper?"

Mr. SALMONIUS: "All right Your Honor. I don't want to do perjury. I did call him an antiman. It is kind-o-fun to see him stutter and get angry."

THIELEY: Mr. Garry Cooper from the Western Front would you be disposed to apologizing to your good friend Mr. Salmonius and say you're sorry for hitting him?

GARRY COOPER: Sir Your Honor Sir. That Mr. Salmoney do that many times and I always promised myself that if I ever catch up with him I would bust him up good: give him a good bussarsing.

THIELEY: You both sure you wont change your minds?

SALMONIUS: Plus Your Honor Sir. He aint name no Garry Cooper. His name is Garry Gunfit.

THIELEY: Never you mind his name. You both still refuse to apologize? Well Mr. Salmonius, as you admitted to calling Mr. Garry Cooper those names I charge you $2.00 for slander. I am glad that I don't have to charge you for perjury. Perjury would add two months time in jail in addition to the $2.00 fine. Now you Mr Garry Cooper from the Western Front, I hereby fine you $2.00 for Aggravated Assault and Battery and 6 months hard labor on the Southern Ranch—Christiansted Pennitentiary.

Normally parties who are ordered by the court to serve more than 2 months are remanded to the Christiansted Pennitentary, St. Croix, south of St. Thomas. At the beginning of each session Judge Thieley reminds Bailiff Carl Wiggley to read that statement.

BETRAYED

Always trusting
Always forgiving
Minimizing cruel and abusive behaviors
Love has no eyes, but
Soft hearts that melt like marsh-mellows at the sound of your voice.
Footsteps that send thrilling sensations as they get closer and closer.
The heart beat harder and faster.
Awaiting the arrival of the king or queen.
"Is this love?" then, I am in love!
AH! a sigh, the truth is told
There is another lover
Demonstrated in the letters secretly tucked away
"Betrayed" the tears fall like rain from a leaking sky
Broken and tormented, unable to sleep, to eat.
Release me from this bondage of pain and suffering
Fly me to freedom
Gaunt and depressed, memories of precious moments
Haunt the soul and boggle the mind
Find a place where peace abound
To calm this broken heart of mine
Do not look back
Be free to find
The love that awaits that I can call mine.

EVERY DAY IS MOTHERS DAY

From the time of conception mothers start nurturing, hugging, talking and singing to their unborn fetus. This is the beginning of the unconditional love, bonding and reciprocal relationship between mothers and children. A mother's love and role are continuous through death.

May 9th, 2004 is designated "mothers day." It is a special day, and a special time of the year when children show their mothers how much they love and appreciate them, and everyone says "Happy Mothers Day." But, everyday should be mother's day. We should always show our appreciation by nurturing, hugging, kissing and telling our mothers how much we love and appreciate them. Send flowers, candies, gift baskets and plants occasionally. This is a nice gesture to show love and appreciation. No matter what you give or the nice things you say, they will always be remembered. Always have a good relationship with your mother.

The bible says "honor thy mother and father that thy days may be long." This is very serious. Think about it.

For those of you who still have your mothers with you, give God the glory.

No child at odds with his/her mother thrives. Make peace now before it's too late.

A Mother's Cry for Help

Ms. May come a calling
Lord all my people are dying
No body answering
No matter what you asking
No body telling
Not even the doctors and nurses reporting
My belly hurting, my body aching
I am constantly crying
Could this be a plaguing?
I need some understanding
All my children and friends are dying
No more name calling or dating
Help me Lord so that I can continue caring
Let me find a place for resting.

DIVING FOR MONEY

People living in the vicinity of the West Indian Company Dock—our deep water port—which accommodate all but the largest tourist pleasure cruisers are those bayside boys, field boys and pollybuggians. We swam out to the large vessels. The passengers tossed coins overboard and we like tractable animals dove and some of us have come away with as much as $3.00 in coins ranging in denominations from a silver dollar, to a half dollar, a quarter a dime or a nickle. We never asked ourselves if these people were really interested in easing our financial burdens. Local St. Thomian divers were mostly among the low class, and aspired to any adventure or work which would improve their lot. Why didn't these tourists ever toss paper money? Were they interested in seeing us dive, to be pleased with our expression of success? For all the years that we dove for coins we never knew of any ulterior motive. Dalton Fatman, AKA Plug Ugly and later Double Ugly was the principal security guard checking autos and trucks, in and out all day long. Double ugly would yell at us while we swam to the ships. While we were there, he said nothing. The days, weeks, months, years rolled by.

A new cop, one of New York's Finest joined the St. Thomas police force. His tour was 8 a.m. to 4.00 p.m....His name was Rex. One day Double Ugly called Rex. Rex came and gained a good and respected rep by running down the fastest guy among us, Raymond Christian. Ray ran through mud. Rex ran through mud. Meanwhile my brother and I tried to bluff Rex while we retrieved our clothing. Earlier Double Ugly and another officer had found our clothes and took them. This time we hid our clothes under a slab of concrete. Rex grabbed us and put us in the green Willies jeep we nicknamed "green wall". After catching Ray—his shoes, socks, and pants foot filled with mud from the refilled land—Rex grabbed the two McFarland brothers.

Of a dozen boys, some Polybuggians and some field boys we had a scenic trip to Fort Christian, straight to Judge Michael Chambers. The order went out to bring parents in. Judge Michael said he would vouch for us since he knew our grandmother, plus we were wearing our clothes…Both McFarland boys were in their birthday suits. Mr McFarland worked twenty minutes away at the Public Works Department. When he arrived he gave the older boy, the brown one his shirt. The red one remained naked. Judge Michael scolded us about the danger of swimming in an area for large ships. Double Ugly asked to give testimony about the danger of diving for money. He started by reminding us of an incident of three months earlier. We all remembered that an 18 year old was slashed by a barracuda and received 28 stitches on his inner left thigh. Dalton continued, "Judge, while the tourists are throwing coins over the side, others were throwing food over the back. Some of them even paid the kitchen help to throw raw meat with the food. The food attract sharks and barracudas and only God knows whatever else. One day one of them is going to get killed."

While we were diving for money all we could think of was getting things our parents and grand parents could use. We were also always occupied with the way the coins moved. The silver dollars, biggest and the heaviest of all, moved in a sideways angle of about 10 degrees. They were the easiest to catch. You simply followed the movement with both hands and by the second or third cycle they were very easy to track and catch. They moved sideways about 18 inches before returning the other 18 inches but they dropped only about 6 inches. The fifty cent coin moved a little faster. They moved sideways about 12 inches and down about 8 inches. The twenty five cents pieces moved sideways about 8 inches back and forth but dropped about 12 inches each time. The nickle moved sideways about 4 to 5 inches but dropped down about 18 inches each time. The dime flickered side to side very quickly. Diving beneath everyone else I could see what each one did. Each one tried to grab the coin with one hand. I was the youngest and had to swim the farthest and the hardest. But I got much more than all the guys together. The ages of the divers ranged from 16 to 70 years. Later they found out that I had gotten more than the lot. They started running me down, wringing my arm behind my back up to my head and taking the money away from me, mostly the Bayside boys. This time I was only 8 years old. Keeping my earnings became an adventure.

They arranged measures to steal my money by setting a person who would hide and wait for me when I left early. My counter measure would be swimming to a part of the dock that was private property, like Yacht Haven or close to Dalton, Double ugly. Even the following day I was fair game and some of them came to the field where I played baseball and tried to strong arm me claiming that I had to split the money with them. Now they were on my turf and the first generation field boys were familiar with their tactics and warded them off. While around the ship diving, some of them tried to run interference to prevent me from getting any money. I used to go to Long Bay and practice speed. All day long I would practice holding my breath until I could stay under water for two minutes.

I learned a bitter lesson doing that. I never realized that using up your supply of oxygen holding your breath made your body less buoyant and your body would start to sink. Not only that, you lose your orientation and can't tell up from down if you cant see the brightness of up. On a sudden overcast day this dilemma hit me and it cost me about a half-a-gallon of water before the cloud passed and I could see the brightness of up. Some of that water went directly into my lungs and the pain—which my grandmother called "Open chest"—remained for six weeks.

Turning Caribbean Tide

The blazing hot Caribbean sun
sending heat waves along the paths
hot enough to cause a sun-stroke
men and women toiled planting sugarcane and cotton
to be reaped and shipped in another six months
that was the industry of the land.
Families were fed and bred and lived well.
Today the Caribbean tide has turned
Tourism is the industry of the land
Everyone look forward to tourist season
and lust at the bodies basking in the hot sun
just for a tan.
Life seems easier, as waiters and waitresses
carry mixed Caribbean drinks to tourists
just vacationing for fun
What if the tourists never come?
Family life will not be fun
Carribbean people should have a back-up plan
Bring back sugar-cane and cotton industry in the land
Stop the total dependence on tourism promotion
Remember life must go on in the Caribbean.

$2.00 JUDGE

Dollar John appeared before Judge Thieley on a charge of Failure to pay child support. Previously Judge Thieley had ordered Dollar John to pay Stupiedie Mary child support of $1.00 monthly. Dollar was picked up on a bench warrant. When Thieley asked Dollar if he did disobey the Court Order Dollar retorted: "yes."

Mr. Dollar John, "said $2.00 Judge Thieley, would you kindly explain to this court why you failed to pay a Court Order duly imposed by this court."?

Said Dollar, "Well Two...."

Said Judge Thieley: "What did you say to me son."?

Said Dollar: "I'm sorry Sir."

Said Judge Thieley: "Address me as Your Honor."

Dollar: Yes Your Honor. Well Your Honor, my refusal has to do with gravity.

$2.00 Thieley: I fail to see how gravity can be blamed for such frivolous treatment of the law.

Dollar: Well Your Honor, Sir, she was standing against the soursop tree."

Thieley: "Continue."

Dollar: Well Your Honor, Sir, she was standing against the soursop tree.

Thieley: "Is that your justification?"

Dollar: "Your what, Sir?"

Thieley: I said address me as Your Honor.

Dollar: Ask Well: Your Honor Sir, 1 too was standing against the same soursop tree, you know

Judge Thieley: What does gravity have to do with your willful disregard to my Court Order?

Dollar: Dammit Two

Thieley: Yelling, his face turning Alizarin Crimson: This Two Holds you in contempt of this court and fines you $2.00. If you carry on this disrespect of this court 1 will have to fine you $2.00 a second time.

Dollar: Well Your Honor Sir, I learned in Manda them School that water nor nothing can go against gravity."

Thieley: What?

Dollar: "Well there you have it. Your Honor Sir"

Thieley: Have What?

Dollar: Well Your Honor Sir, when I broke all the spence run back out, down hill just like they taught me in Manda them school

Thieley: Well, Mr. Dollar, this court is here to inform you and others like you that water not only can go uphill but over the hill with enough force and I am sure you use sufficient force to make that child. You are hereby reordered to make up the $12.00 you missed. This court now orders you to pay $2.00 a month. If you come back to this court I'll lock you up for two years while you pay your $2,00 and are released to attend Manda School to re-learn about gravity.

A BROKEN HEART

My heart breaks

As I watched HIV/AIDS cause your body to ache The smiles you try to fake

To make life a bit easier to take

Through the pain and suffering you forget your treatment date

As I watched you whither away

I pray for peace and understanding for God's sake

Help me to understand this HIV/AIDS outbreak

Dear Lord tell me what to create

To end this pandemic state.

HOPE FOR TOM

HIV/AIDS cause illnesses that make Tom lame
Multiple antiretroviral drugs that are never the same
When will he be free from all this drug regimen
Ah! he is unable to move: weakness, neuropathy again
Another drug regimen in vane
How much longer will his misery remain
Isn't this a shame?
He is constantly in pain
Should he give up and perish or start a new drug regimen?
Ah! he proclaims reclaim. The new regimen work again.

Can a court lie?

While on vacation in my home, St. Thomas, Virgin Islands, I stopped at the sub-base tennis courts. Among the many old friends that I met was Robert, known in my family as "Robert 'd Owl." The other guys listened as Robert and I reminisced about fishing together, Robert 12 years my senior. Roberts' knowledge about Virgin Islands news and folklore is commendable and he reminded me of many things I thought that I had forgotten. The conversation went from one topic to another fluently and several of the others contributed to the discussion, including Dr. Sprauve. I made a new re-acquaintance with a former student who is now a college professor of Music, Jazz pianist Louis Taylor. Naturally with two musicians, music became the bottom line. The conversation shifted to the Man who owned the Music store Back Street, Radaats Gade—Alan Grammer.

Immediately the statement was made and seconded that Grammer was a racist Some of the guys were so dogmatic about Grammer being a racist that I had to approach the topic with an overkill. The information I know about Alan Grammer is not known by any of the guys present and I doubt that any one else but Frankie Jarvis knows this story. It was revealed to a small circle. Grammer however is not a subject of Virgin Island parlor conversation.

Frankie Jarvis, a drummer, and his wife Lisa were very good friends of the Grammers. Lisa called Grammer's wife Beasley. They exchanged visits. During the time of the incident which branded Grammer as a racist I was an undergraduate student of Music (English and Secondary Education) at Inter-American University in San German, Puerto Rico. On between semesters or trimesters visits home, I met and came to know and respect Grammer greatly through Frankie, not only as a very competent musician, but as a mentor, a fellow who practiced with the virgin Islands Community Band, and a fellow who got me involved for many years in visiting Radio Station WSTA to play Christmas Carols on the air, both of us playing slide trombones, Gus on the Baritone saxophone and a fourth trumpeter whose name presently escapes me. Grammer was the one who introduced me to the Community Band; and to playing Christmas Carols at WSTA.

I had practiced with the Community Band at least thrice, and each time Grammer and I stopped at a bar downstairs from the second floor where the Community Band rehearsed. This night Frankie Jarvis was present. Until this time I had not heard about Grammer being a racist or losing his liquor license in a controversial court case.

In walked Curtis Callender, a Sanitation Inspector, dressed in his khaki sanitation uniform. I knew Curtis for lappy arse years as the oldest of four brilliant brothers, Holland, Wilbur and Caswell. Grammer, the elder, had bought Frankie and me the first round of Heineken beers. Curtis ordered the second round of beers. Frankie and I accepted beers. Grammer declined. Curtis seemed insistant on ordering the third round. Grammer declined a second time. This second time I sensed attitude. Then Callendar dropped the bomb.

Straight to the point, Callendar, uncontested, uninterrupted, said: "Hi man. I am sorry that I caused you to lose your license. I am sorry, but you must forgive me because I was drunk; I was totally out of It" On our way home, Frankie Jarvis told me the story of the court case in which Judge Gordon relieved Alan Grammer of his liquor license. Subsequently Grammer told me that Curtis had been a regular patron; that he knew Curtis very well—one of the reasons Curtis patronized Grammer's Bar. Grammer said he was serving a white female client and Curtis walked in and demanded to be served immediately. Having dealt with Curtis times before, drunk and sober, Grammer did as he always did with Curtis. He told him to hold his horses. Curtis' Boisterousness caused a patron to call the cops.

I wondered if over the years had Curtis made a connection between his benign neglect and Grammer's death?

Has anyone made any connection between Grammer's death and the recent skyjacking? Comes to mind the lesson Shakespeare teaches in "Macbeth:" The first murder, the first lie, always leads to a second. Curtis enabled the first lie by benign neglect. The Territorial Court committed the second in suggesting to Curtis not to appear. In effect the case became: "The State (Territorial Court) vs. Grammer." Curtis knew that his behavior caused a supposed friend to lose his liquor license and did nothing about it. He became committed to the court lie.

For me this situation has been extremely painful. It's commendable that the island would protect its own. But Alan Grammer was as much "its own" as curtis. Grammer helped more local people than Curtis did. Grammer was as much a part of the community as Curtis. As a matter of fact, Grammer practiced as a trombonist with our Community Band. Grammer was the one who invited me to practice with the Community Band. Grammer was the one who invited me to play Christmas Carols at WSTA. Grammer helped more local fledgling musicians than anyone else I know at no cost. Grammer did much to advance my music career.

I am certain that Curtis would agree with me that the Government should erect a monument to Alan Grammer as one of the Virgin Islands solid citizen. I had to write this story because I heard my friends pronounce, judge and were willing to execute him, which is exactly what led to his wrongful death. Take it from me. Alan Grammer was as much a racist as Curtis Callendar. Grammer had no 'ace-in-the-hole' like a list of 22 names of the Virgin Islands most active faggots to fend-off being railroaded and couldn't threaten the Territorial Court otherwise. He received a double death: the first was his livelihood; the second was his life.

The Virgins Island Government should right this wrong, if only for his family's sake and posterity. It would go a long way to help the image of the U.S. Virgin Islands facing the prospect of improving the tourist trade. Let's show that we are mature enough to let the family down easy and do something visible to assuage our cousins. Governor Charles Wesley Turnbull is one of the most brilliant men I know. Let him think of something. St. Croix could use this opportunity to improve its image.

A VIRAL ENCOUNTER
HIV/AIDS AND WORLD DISTRUCTION

The world is being destroyed not by fire and not by water
The world is being destroyed by a pandemic that we encounter
   Was it manufactured by a virus from a computer?
The CDC says we must use condoms and abstinence to protect
   us from this viral danger.
God tells us to multiply and reproduce, yet there are
   Decreased births and increased deaths.
   The world is being reduced
   HIV/AIDS has caused this recluse.
   Pain and sorrow sting like a dagger
   Afraid to romance and caress our lover
   We cannot run, we cannot hide
   HIV/AIDS is whipping our hide
   We must all take a stance
   Just don't sit by the wayside and glance?
Together we can fight to eradicate this HIV/AIDS killer virulence.

THE STREET FIGHTER

Pat McGlobey was a disgruntled Negro U.S. Marine dishonorably discharged after two demotions with bad time in the brig. He is a Long Path boy who never returned home and was trained in Mr. Andre's mechanic shop, Glass Bottle Alley, just below Lincoln School steps. He was incessantly mouthing-off about: "Whitey this, Whitey that, and if he had the will of Whitey what he would do." He fancied himself an extra-ordinary street fighter and was always getting into scraps. Even as a boy in Longpath, when the word went out the: "Pat is fighting; which one, the white one or the black one? His record of accosting superior officers attest to his belief in his fighting prowess. He was always bragging how Uncle Sam trained him.

His record of the plethora of defeats and injuries he sustained told a totally different storey. In the days just before the two liter glass soda bottle bit the dust, a teenager broke a bottle on his head. A Dominican planarsed him with a cutlash and broke all the bones in his hand. The amazing fact that he would have you believe is that he was supposed to be trained to assist in rescue missions behind enemy lines. His descriptions about using a piano wire with two wooden handles to decapitate an enemy, stabbing an enemy just below the sacral dimple to silence him, etc., was impressive, but after a while I thought he was storey.

On his last job as a truck mechanic, he hired two junkies (Paid each $10.00) to travel all the way out to long Island, N.Y to beat up his boss. They beat the boss up only to have him report back to the job the next day bright and early.

One day after his continuous spiel about "Whitey," I dressed him down about the shit he was talking. I told him about an old friend of mine named Juanito Leonard Denton in St. Thomas. Denton was a well-known man and his place of business was one of the most popular for men seeking gaming pleasure. His pool room had six 4 by 8 tables and one 5 by 9. They were always busy. Several back rooms made dice and cards accessible at $2.00 a head each hand. He had one of the first TV's in his dance hall from 1954—a 25" color Admiral. Imagine the numerous bouts that Denton had with some of his clients: local boys, marines, sailors, other tourists, etc. I told Pat McGlobey about many of the tricks that Denton told me he had learned over the years.

As the story goes the U. S. Military was in, sailors and marines. Most times returning military was dropped off at the West Indian Company Dock. Denton was a hacker at night and had a fare of 4 marines. Because the harbor was filled, these returning marines had to be taken to the waterfront to be ferried out to their ship moored outside the harbor. A brown-skinned, cooley haired marine yelled at Denton: "Hi you arrogant black West Indian bastard, let's see you take your money how you can." Denton reached under his car seat and retrieved the tail end of a pool cue and moved toward the four marines. The same marine feigned a blow to Denton's face. Naturally Denton raised his hand up to protect his face. The marine stooped down rapidly grabbing Denton's pants foot on the inside—near his inner ankles—and heaved him over his car. Denton landed on the other side of his car, feet first. This was planned by these marines who were a team of ranked fighters for their ship. Denton was unhurt and surprised that the men were all laughing not at him but with him. The ranked wrestler who heaved him over the car said: "We just wanted to see just how good you were. Like most people with a cudgel in a fight almost always—exclusively—go first for the face. That's a mistake. I faked you high and went low. It works every time. You think you got that?"

Denton was very serious at first. The only thing on his mind was his fare, but after he got it, he stood there a while and gaffed with the four marines. The following evening he had more business than he could use. Year later various ships carrying marines who heard of the famous Denton's Bar, Restaurant and Pool Hall patronized his place of business. I told him many other stories Denton had told me about getting an edge in street fighting.

Weeks later I received a call from Pat McGlobey foreday morning about 3:00 a.m. I had received calls from him at this time before. Pat drove a Checker cab at nights when jobs were scarce. It's almost like history repeating itself. Pat said to me over the phone: "The ting wok."

"What ting wok?"

"The ting from Denton."

"Oh, that. Well what happened?"

"I picked up a tall black fare with a small skinny woman; took them all the way to New Jersey. This guys tells me: You West Indian people come here and make all the money. You are a bunch of opportunistic bastards. I ain payin you."

I pulled out from under my seat a two foot length of three-quarter inch black pipe with a cap on the end. I faked him to the head and he went for it. I know I broke he shin bone. Boy he curled up like a dead cockroach bawling like a child. He pulled out a roll of money and begged me like I was his father: Take it all only please don't hit me again, Please!

"How much did you take?"

"After a quick check seeing at least five $20's, I know that this roll covered the fare. I got about three hundred on a $120.00 fare. Not bad, eh?"

PAT MCGLOBEY THE MATCHMAKER

American citizenship is a very valuable asset to aliens seeking a better life in the United States. Pat McGlobey designed a business venture to offer American citizenship to women of the Caribbean. He offered $2000.00 to an American West Indian male to marry an alien woman and charged the female $5000.00 for the privilege of becoming an American citizen. His first couple consisted of an Antiguan female called "Babey" and a West Indian American citizen called "Puddin."

After McGlobey prompted the couple on how to pass the Immigration test on familiarity—such as knowing some major likes and dislikes about each other, Babey and Puddin got married. Puddin got his first $1000.00 and as agreed; he was to get another thousand dollars at the end of the first year after the agreed upon divorce. Time marched on and at the end of the first year Puddin approached Babey for the second $1000.00.

Meanwhile Puddin and Babey became infatuated with each other and Babey allowed Puddin to move into her apartment. During the year Babey had become accustomed to preparing meals for Puddin. Puddin brought home his check to Babey who took care of the household finances. Before the year was up Babey gave birth to Puddin's baby girl.

Babey reviewed all the privileges Puddin got living in her apartment, eating her cooking and most importantly, fathering her baby girl.

Before Puddin became a loving husband, doting father and responsible citizen, he was the fourth hand in a poker clotch. His recent conflict with Babey caused him much embarrassment and revived his wanderlust. At the same time he was seen by one of his old poker buddies who promptly invited him to resume his regular spot at the poker table. All his old buddies knew him to work as a security guard at Kinneys, 444 Madison Avenue. Dejected and despondent he appeared at his old haunt at 116th at "The Hole," a very popular St. Thomian hangout in New York for the past 60 years.

'Til now Puddin hadn't had a drink for almost a year. It was a regular Friday, payday night, and whereas he was considered the luckiest poker player, this Friday night he lost his entire paycheck. He had become very diligent in handing over his paycheck to Babey. This Friday night he got home not only broke but as high as a kite on the hunt

Babey didn't give him a chance to explain, for over their year together Puddin had filled Babey's ear with his old carousing, gambling and womanizing. She didn't need any explanation. As she was the youngest child of five children, the first four being bully boys in a West Indian (Antiguan) culture, she had become very adept a fisticuffs, minus Marquis of Queensbury. Puddin's attempt to uphold his status as "Head of Household" didn't impress Babey. His claim to wearing the pants in the family didn't set well with Babey either. A fight erupted, Babey prevailed with a left/right combination followed very quickly with a hip throw. Babey's account of the conflict claims that she immediately drew his lead-loaded billy club and it was "Good Night Gracey."

Babey called Pat Mcglobey right away and in a low, calm tone said over the phone: "McGlob, I think I killed Puddin." McGlobey asked her if she had called the police. The answer was, "No," McGlob told her not to call the cops and to wait for him.

When McGlob got over to Babey's apartment, he found Puddin comatose with very small bubbles at the corners of his mouth, no pulse and a hell of a lump over his carotid artery. Babey was an LPN at Lincoln Memorial in the Bronx and had a certificate in CPR, but she didn't try it until McGlobey showed up—too late. For about two hours they tried to revive Puddin, mostly by dashing water in his face but to no avail. This whole donnybrook started about 11:00 p.m. Friday night and McGlobey called me 2:30 a.m. Saturday.

Pat McGlobey said over the phone: I think Babey killed Puddin and I need you to help me get rid of the body. I protested, objected and cursed him (swore at) 'til he said: "Alright, calm down. I'll try to get someone else. Just stand by the phone. I reminded him that it wasn't the wisest thing to say what he said over the phone. He agreed and hung up.

My computer went into 'fast forward,' then 'search', then 'overdrive.' I thought about the wet uniform, the water, stuffing the body in an abandoned carapace and all sorts of help aids. Then it slowed down rapidly and came to a halt. I reminded myself that: under no circumstance would I get involved with a homicide. I didn't get any of the $3000,00 Pat McGlobey made. All the help I ever received from him related to fixing my Buick Le Sabre, which I gave him with one full year of insurance. Plus he ran up $1500.00 in parking violations. I owed him nothing.

The phone rang about 5:00 a.m. Pat McGlobey said: We found Puddin sitting up in the bedroom, so you don't need to be concerned.

UPON ARISING SUN, A SETTING SUN, A RISING MOON

The day breaks
The cocks crow. Its 3:00 a.m.
Fishermen awaken and prepare for the catch of the day
Contractors load their trucks
Hoping to build their masterpiece high on a hill
Motorists slowly moving
The roads communicate at the sound of increasing speed
The noise gets louder and louder
Another day, another dollar
The sun shines brighter and brighter
People hustle and bustle on crowded streets
Alas! The calm is restored
The sun has done its job for the day
Tiredly it creeps behind the horizon
Reflecting a flare of gold on the ocean bed
Resting, energizing to gain strength for another day
Sinking deeper and deeper
Night falls and darkness consumes the land
Suddenly the moon peeks over the hilltops
As if to say, "here I am to brighten your night"
Lovers walk hand in hand
Enjoying the moonlit skies and the cool Caribbean breeze
No problem, no need to fan.

978-0-595-33257-1
0-595-33257-9